Before I Got In!

The Young Teen's College Audition Guide for Acting and Musical Theatre

Mary Anna Dennard

Acknowledgments

Special thanks to my former parents who advocate the importance of early preparation to ensure success in the college audition process. I am eternally grateful for your valuable contributions to this book, and for your continued participation in our extended theatre family. And thanks to my trusted friend and able assistant, "Normal" Nancy Marston.

To my former, current and future students:

Be Joyous, because you love this

Be Brave, because you are fierce

Be Yourself, because you are enough....

And as Oscar Wilde said,
"Be yourself. Everyone else is already taken"

About the Author

Mary Anna's first book, *I GOT IN! The Ultimate College Audition Guide For Acting And Musical Theatre*, was featured in the New York Times where she was a special contributor to the Theatre Section's Artsbeat blog.

She received her training at The American Conservatory Theater in San Francisco, before working as a casting director and acting coach in Los Angeles in the 1980s. Her fifteen years of casting credits have garnered Clios, Emmys, Academy Awards, and a Peabody Award.

Since 2000, she has been a college audition coach for programs in acting and musical theater. In 2011, she founded the first-ever online prep for performing arts college applicants, collegeauditioncoach.com

As a nationally recognized expert in her field, Mary Anna has coached hundreds of students from all over the country, who have been accepted into the most prestigious college training programs in the United States and Europe. Her former students have gone on to have successful careers after college in the recording industry, on television, in motion pictures, and on Broadway.

She conducts master classes throughout the country and serves as a guest instructor for the Broadway Dreams Foundation, Broadway Teachers Workshop, the Dallas Summer Musicals, and The Performing Arts Project.

Follow her regular college blog in the Huffington Post. And visit her website, collegeauditioncoach.com.

Contents

Acknowledgments 3
About the Author... 6
Introduction 11

Chapter One: Getting Started... 13
School Involvement 13
Copies of Your Performances 14
Acceptd 15
Outside of School... 15
Dance 15
Acting 16
Voice... 17
Piano... 17
Competitions 18
Summer Enrichment 18
Camp or Precollege 19
Monologues 20

Chapter Two: College Audition Timeline 23
Sophomore Year 23
Summer after sophomore year 23
Junior Year 24
Second semester of junior year 24
Summer after junior year 25
Senior year 26

Chapter Three: Research College Programs 29
College visits 30

Performing Arts Degrees 33
BA, BFA, BM, Conservatory 34
Reaches, Fits, and Safeties 36
A Smart List 37

Chapter Three: College Audition Requirements 39
Requirements 39
Monologues 39
Songs...41
Dance Combination 42
Music Theory Test 42

Chapter Four: The Academic Component..............43
Get ready by asking yourself questions 44
Grades 44
Course selection 44
Academics and scholarships 45
Test Prep 45
Letters of Recommendation 46
Volunteer Work 46

Chapter Five: Mock Auditions and Master Classes 47

Chapter Six: Performance Resume and Headshot 51
Your Resume 51
Your Headshot..53

Chapter Seven: Audition Locations 57
On-Campus Auditions 57
Off-Campus Auditions 57
Consortium Auditions 58
National Unified Auditions 59
Prescreen Audition 60
Digital Audition 61

Chapter Eight: Mental Preparation 63
FOR PARENTS 64
FOR STUDENTS.. 66

Chapter Nine: College Acceptances.. 71
Acceptances 72
Rejections 72
Deferrals/Waitlists 72
Accepting an Offer 73

Chapter Ten: College Audition Coaching 75
My Coaching 77

Conclusion 79
If I Knew Then, What I Know Now 81
General Advice 81
For those specifically interested in musical theatre 84

.. ..89
Summer Performing Arts Programs 91
Colleges Offering Degrees in
Acting and Musical Theater 98

Introduction

We live in an accelerated world. Basketball players are taller, swimmers are faster, weight lifters are stronger, and figure skaters routinely land a triple Lutz. High frequency trading has hit the stock market, three year-olds want iPads for Christmas, and tweens can sing like *American Idol.* It should come as no surprise that more and more families are contacting me asking what they can do for their fourteen year-old thespain to prepare for college auditions.

This prompted me to write a guide for the families of high school freshmen and sophomores to help them prepare for the performing arts college admission process.

I have entitled it, *Before I GOT IN! The Young Teen's College Audition Guide for Acting And Musical Theatre.* This new guide serves as a prequel to my popular first book, *I GOT IN! The Ultimate College Audition Guide For Acting And Musical Theatre.*

I GOT IN! was the first book of its kind, and with this prequel, I offer another first. (Ironically, in reverse order)

If you believe that the serious study of acting and musical theatre is in your child's future, this young teen's guide will lay the groundwork for what is to come. Although it may be too early to know for certain the level of your child's interest, chances are you already know if the passion for performing is there.

Chapter One

Getting Started

School Involvement

It is important for hopeful thespians to involve themselves in their high school theatre and drama programs. Find out about all the performance opportunities that are available in your school. At a large public school, this can be a challenge. Typical opportunities include: school plays and musicals, drama class, forensic competitions, choir, show choir, speech class, University Interscholastic League (UIL) competition, arts festivals and state thespian conventions that you enter via your high school drama club. Your teachers and counselors as well as older students and friends can advise you about how to become a member of these clubs and organizations, in addition to any school auditions. Many of the performing arts schools are going to have more classes, shows and clubs available. But even if you live in a small town or go to a small school, there will be classes you can take and ways you can participate to show your interest within your school.

Here is some advice from an experienced high school public school drama teacher about the level of involvement she suggests for the early high school years to prepare students for college theatre studies.

"The best preparation for younger students is to take as many theater classes as you can. But if your school doesn't offer theater, consider speech and oral interp to help with memorization skills and performing before a judge. If your school does offer theater, take the class, and learn all you can. Remember that when you go to college you will be taking with you all the building blocks you have developed from high school. This is how to start to build your "creative house". High school is your foundation and without a strong foundation, you won't be as competitive in your early years of college. And learn to love auditioning. Do it all you can. In my opinion every audition is a chance to grow and learn. If you are an underclassman and don't get cast, find a way to be involved so that you can learn from the sidelines. Stage managing, assistant directing and running crew get you right into the mix of things. You can learn so much by watching. Most of all start thinking about the future. You don't have to decide where you are going to college as a high school freshman, but do early research and learn about college theatre programs. Talk to your theater teachers, speech teacher and forensics coach. They are going to walk side by side with you on the path to college. They are there to help you. Keep learning and growing, and keep your passion alive!"

Copies of Your Performances

And here is a note from me: Be sure you get digital copies of all your performances, and archive them. You may need to use the clips later to submit to colleges and summer performing arts programs as a supplement to your application and/or auditions. You will be surprised how they can come in handy if a performance sample is requested. When I consult with families, I often request any video footage they might have available so that I can assess the skill level of the student. So keep footage of yourself dancing, singing and acting. You may need it later.

Acceptd

If you want to begin to archive and organize your digital media online, open a dashboard on acceptd, a performing arts applicant management site that hosts student actors video clips. It is free to have a dashboard, and you can use it to submit summer performing arts program audition videos. Later when you apply to colleges, your acceptd profile will be the place where you send college applications and video prescreens for many of the college programs. So it would be handy to begin your acceptd profile now. The website is listed in the Resources section.

Outside of School

You may already be taking private instruction outside of school in voice, dance, piano or other musical instruments as well as acting classes. I encourage you to continue your classes.

One of the keys to getting ready for your college auditions is to begin your training now so you can perform at a competitive level once the audition process begins in your senior year. An ideal way to get prepared is to take private or group classes outside of school, in your community.

Dance

If you are going to pursue musical theater, it is very important that you get in dance lessons right away. Especially you guys! Your dance skills could make the difference in whether you get an offer of acceptance over another applicant. It is likely that you took dance in elementary school or middle school and may have had to cut back on classes for various reasons. If that is the case, it is time to get back in class. And I recommend ballet above all other styles. If you read my book, *I GOT IN!* you know that I say, "Ballet is to dance

what Latin is to language". Ballet is the basis of all dance styles, and
the college dance combos that you will be given for musical theater
auditions will include choreography that is based in ballet technique.
So ballet is the best thing you can be doing now to get ready, and I
recommend three ballet lessons a week. This may get more difficult
as you get more active in the upper classes at your high school, but it
is very important that you keep your dance up if you want to pursue
musical theater at the college level. You might consider teaming up
with some of your performer friends and scheduling semi-private
ballet classes with a local dance instructor, as your schedule permits.
And again, I cannot stress this enough for guys.

Acting

It is likely that you live in a city where there are opportunities to
perform in your community Also, there may be acting classes in your
community that are conducted by professional actors. These classes
may be available to young teens, and will be enormously important
in your development as an actor. You can contact the local theatre
in your area and inquire, or search online.

This could include: community theatre, community centers,
outreach programs, after school enrichment classes, performing arts
camps, churches, temples or local professional theatres. Look into
these outlets as a participant, or even a volunteer or intern. All of
these opportunities outside of your classroom are things that you
should be pursuing at this early high school stage. As you take acting
classes always be on the lookout for monologue material that suits
your age and experience. You will always need monologues for
auditions that come up along the way.

Voice

Of course, if you're going to pursue musical theater you need to have a voice teacher who can assess you vocally and give you vocal technique lessons. It is an absolute necessity that a knowledgeable and experienced vocal teacher assesses you early. This will protect your vocal health and insure that you are receiving correct instruction. You will also need to start building "your book". This is what we refer to as your book of rep, or book of song repertoire. The songs contained in your book may be those you are working on with your voice teacher, or may come from another source familiar with the musical theatre canon. It is important that your instructor is current in their knowledge of musical theatre songs as well as those of different styles within musical theatre. You want the songs in your book to be songs you love to sing, can easily sing (even on a bad day) that show off your vocal strengths and hide your vocal weaknesses. Your song rep is going to be part of your personal development as a vocalist.

Piano

And, for musical theatre, it's an excellent idea to take piano lessons now. Learning about sight reading music and learning about music theory, and beginning to learn how to play the piano well is an integral part of the well-rounded musical theatre performer. More and more colleges are interested in applicants who have proficiency in a musical instrument. So even if you do not take piano, proficiency in any musical instrument will be beneficial. You may be in your school band or orchestra, or play the guitar as a hobby Keep it up. It will really pay off for you later.

Competitions

There are other ways to grow and perform that include performance competitions. These competitions (some are national) are excellent opportunities for you to see how your talents measure up to the other students. These are the kids that you will ultimately be competing against for spots in the performing arts colleges. I have mentioned the UIL school sponsored competitions, but there are plenty of national arts organizations that offer competitions outside of your high school. These include the National YoungArts Foundation competition (this leads to the Presidential Scholar nominees), National Association of Teachers of Singing (NATS) competition or the National Shakespeare Competition sponsored by the English-Speaking Union. Another reason to participate in these competitions is that there can be sizeable prize money attached to the award. I have listed these websites in the back of this book under Resources.

Summer Enrichment

The good news is there seems to be an ever-growing number of summer performing arts enrichment opportunities. I think the first thing you want to ask yourself before researching a summer program is what you want to gain out of your summer experience. Exactly what kind of program do you want to attend? There are so many different types of programs out there that the best thing to do is to start with what you want. There are probably opportunities for you to perform in the summer in local programs. Those camps can be a fun way to spend your summer and stay close to home. But if you look nation-wide for programs, you will find more summer opportunities from which to choose.

Camp or Precollege

If you are a freshman or sophomore, and have not experienced being away from home for an extended length of time, you might be more comfortable staying in your community and enrolling in some sort of performing arts *camp*. If you are interested in a lot of stage time, ask the program if they do a full production at the end of the term. Or, the camp may produce something more like a revue or recital styled performance on the last day.

There are also *precollege* summer enrichment programs for the performing arts. These types of offerings might be what you want to consider the summer before your junior year or even the summer before your senior year. Precollege summer programs provide the opportunity to study on a campus, stay in a dorm and be taught by college professors. This experience can be very valuable as you get older and into your senior year.

Whether you decide on camps or precollege programs, both have long lasting benefits because you will be learning more about your craft, developing your abilities and practicing your performance skills. Each program operates their registration differently. Some summer programs are going to require you to audition. These auditions generally begin in January or before. Often you can submit a digital audition with your application if an in-person audition is not convenient. Other programs do not require an audition. I have included an extensive list it in the back of the book under Resources. I would encourage you to investigate the offerings, but not until you have talked as a family about what it is you want your experience to be. Another consideration would be cost. Some of these programs are very expensive. But if you inquire, you may find that some offer full or partial scholarships for those that qualify.

Monologues

Okay, I'm going to break this down for you. Your college audition evaluation will be based on Acting (for acting programs), or Acting, Singing and Dancing (for musical theatre programs). I want to bring special focus on the monologue, because ALL your auditions will require a monologue or monologues for the acting portion. I have found that most young performers are clueless when it comes to choosing monologues. So, what can you be doing now to help prepare for your college audition monologues? Read on, my friends.

The first thing you need to do is attend the theater regularly. Go to see plays at your school, and/or be in them if you can. And attend community theatre in your neighborhood. Another idea, and one that I personally enjoy, is to see plays in other towns when you're traveling, or on vacation. But most important of all is to read plays. You need to be reading plays all the time. Learn about new playwrights that interest you and learn about the different styles of writing and the different styles and different genres of plays and playwrights. A good way to find new plays is to read the *New York Times* theatre section and read *Playbill* and *Backstage*. I have them bookmarked on my computer and read them every day. Also, the Drama Book Shop, Samuel French and Dramatists Play Service are just some of the excellent resources for scripts. There are many more, and you can find them if you search online. There are a variety of periodicals including *American Theater Magazine* where you can learn about new works that are being produced and new playwrights. Also, you should subscribe to *Dramatics Magazine*. It is published by the Educational Theatre Association, and will help you stay current with what is new in the world of high school theatre. You can also familiarize yourself with play titles by going to various theater companies' websites and seeing what plays they're producing, and what their season is.

Reading plays and publications about theatre is something you need to start now so you are empowered with knowledge about plays, playwrights and theatrical productions. This is the biggest problem I see in my coaching business. Young actors do not know enough about plays and playwrights, or how to find monologues. You can do something about that now, by following my suggestions.

Chapter Two

College Audition Timeline

Sophomore Year

Continue to perform and study. Your classes should include voice and dance, if you are anticipating pursuing musical theatre. Keep adding credits to your resume. Participate in as many school sponsored theatre and performance opportunities as possible. Stay involved in outside performing arts. Go to the theatre and read plays.

If you are on family vacations, you might stop by some college campuses within driving distance, to get the feel of campus life. Arrange for a tour of the college theatre, if possible. But I advise against expensive college visits at this early stage. Save that for later during junior and senior year.

Summer after sophomore year

Attend a performing arts summer camp or precollege intensive. Explore programs outside your local area so that you can expand your knowledge of instructors and students from a national pool. This will ready you for the competition you are likely to face during the college audition season and introduce you to new experiences. I have an excellent list of summer programs in the Resources section at the back of this book.

Junior Year

Begin to ask yourself and your parents, "What kind of college is best for you?" List the six most important things you are looking for in a college. I call these your "Must-Haves". Enter three for the training program in your major, and three for the university experience. Must-haves might include: BA or BFA, student body size, study abroad options, senior showcase, performance opportunities as an underclassman, strong emphasis on acting, tuition limitations, location, etc.

For more examples of university and program criteria, refer to Interview Questions in *I GOT IN!* This will help you to begin thinking about what you want to focus on in your college search. You must know what you want before you can know what colleges to apply to.

Make plans to attend the free National Association For College Admission Counseling (NACAC) Performing Arts College Fair in your area. Check their schedule to see if the fair will be in a city near you. Their web address is in the back of this book in the Resources section. At the fair, you can meet with theatre representatives from over eighty colleges and learn about their programs. Ask specific questions to see how they match up with your must-haves.

Begin going online to visit the various performing arts programs on the college websites. Look at their show season, curriculum and faculty. Take a virtual tour.

Second semester of junior year

Begin researching college audition coaches, to help you in the process. Search online or ask around to see if there is an experienced coach in your area. Be sure the coach has a proven record of success with college auditions, specifically. It is very common nowadays to begin working with a coach outside your city or town using Internet video conferencing via Skype, FaceTime or Google Hangout. I typically begin coaching students and prepping for college auditions in the spring of junior year. College audition coaches' hourly fees can vary from $75 to $200.

Summer after junior year

Attend a precollege performing arts summer program. Many colleges and universities offer these types of summer intensives that can last from one week to six weeks. You might prefer a summer program on the campus one of the schools you are interested in attending. A list of these summer programs is in the Resources section. These types of programs can have a hefty price tag. If you are not able to do a precollege program, I recommend that you continue your studies, classes and performance opportunities in your area. Volunteer or work as an intern at a local arts camp or community theatre. And continue to attend the theatre and read plays!

If you have hired a coach, this should be the time you begin final work on preparing your audition material and begin to finalize your college list. Participate in master classes to try out your material in a mock setting and get feedback from the college representatives. Get to know the colleges and faculty members who will be auditioning you. Available master classes can be found on my website Store page at collegeauditioncoach.com. Or you can do a search on the Internet to find additional master audition offerings. I have more information on master classes in Chapter five.

Senior year

Stay in close contact with your college audition coach. Review college audition requirements and time limits on the college websites. Finalize your audition material and college list. Actors, finalize your classical and contemporary monologues. Musical Theatre students, ready your monologues, song choices, book of rep and cuts, and take ballet class three times a week!

Begin the college application process with the assistance of your parents, high school counselor or independent advisor. Check for schools that accept the common application. The common app website is on the Resources page.

October

Record your electronic prescreens for the colleges that require them. Follow instructions exactly. You do not need to hire a professional videographer. Use a high quality digital camera, if possible. Or if you plan to use a mobile device, be sure it shoots in HD. Have a plain background, good lighting and sound. If singing, be sure your voice can be heard clearly above the accompaniment. I have an excellent instructional video on how to shoot your prescreen. It is available on my website Store page. I highly recommend it. When you have completed shooting your prescreens, upload them to Acceptd or Decision Desk, the third party applicant management sites.

The results of your prescreens with come in the weeks following your submission via the third party applicant site where you uploaded the prescreen, or from the college itself.

Have your headshot and resume completed, and audition outfit chosen.

November

Begin plotting your audition schedule and making travel plans. If you are using my online prep membership, you will have use of the online Audition Master Planner. But you can create your own audition schedule with an Excel spreadsheet. Keep up-to-date files on each school. Continue to participate in mock auditions and master classes. You will be very busy with college prep, so I advise that you not get too over scheduled with school performances.

November-March College Auditions begin!

Many of the college auditions are conducted on-campus. However, about 50 colleges hold regional auditions during the National Unified Auditions. National Unified dates and locations can be found on their website which is listed under Resources in this book. The Unified cities include: New York, Chicago, Las Vegas and Los Angeles. Unified audition dates begin in late January and continue until late February. Attending Unifieds is a great way to complete several auditions in one location. I have written more on Unifieds in chapter seven, College Audition Locations.

April

Sort out your acceptances/deferrals/ waitlists/rejections. Visit ALL schools to which you have been accepted. Compare scholarships/tuition.

May 1st

This is the national reply-by date. You must make your final college decision by this date and have placed your deposit.

Chapter Three
Research College Programs

Sophomore year is not too soon to begin researching college programs. There are over one hundred of them. And if you start now and take it slowly, you will find that you can learn quite a bit from the Internet, if you just begin looking at some of the programs I have listed at the back of my book. One of the best ways you can begin your college research is to visit one of the NACAC Visual and Performing Arts College Fairs that may be coming to a town where you live. NACAC is an acronym for the National Association of College Admissions Counseling. It is important that you get started now researching and studying the various college performing arts programs. I give you a lot of information in this chapter, but you will need to take this information and do your own investigation. Be diligent and take good notes. College websites are full of details and data that will help you in your information gathering. And there are additional related online resources at your disposal. I have included the most helpful ones here.

When you are a junior, you can begin to compile your college list. The (NACAC) Performing And Visual Arts College Fair travels to seventeen cities throughout the United States beginning in the fall. The fair is free and an excellent way to meet with college representatives from the theater and musical theater university programs. There are as many as eighty colleges that participate in the fair. You can find their Web site under Resources at the end of this book.

Most traditional college fairs include representatives from the college's general admissions office, and they know little about the theater programs. The NACAC Performing Arts College Fair is different because the representatives are experts in their college's theater admissions process and can answer most any questions you have. You can learn about educational opportunities, admission and financial aid, audition and entrance requirements, and much more by meeting with representatives from colleges, universities, conservatories, festivals, and other educational institutions with specialized programs in the visual arts and performing arts.

It is a good idea for parents and students to attend together. Get there early. Go with an organized list of schools that interest you. Write down questions for the colleges, and take detailed notes. The NACAC Performing Arts College Fair is usually crowded and can be somewhat overwhelming. But if you are well organized, it can be a very productive information- gathering session. It will definitely aid you in focusing your college list. It is best if you attend your sophomore or junior year.

College visits

In addition to NACAC, the college websites are very comprehensive. Many of them have virtual tours so you can actually take a virtual look at the school and the campus and you may email the admissions office and the theatre programs are all very approachable and friendly and can answer any questions you have about the program. In addition to this, you may find that you want to do some early campus visits. I have a pretty strong opinion that it is not a good idea to spend a lot of money taking campus visits early in your high school years. Traveling is very expensive its very disruptive to your family if you have parents that are working, and you are in school. However if you find you are already taking a family vacation and you are going to be in the New York area and you want to go visit a couple of colleges that are in the Northeast then that's probably a fine idea. But I wouldn't spend a lot of money giving campus visits early on. I would wait and do that later in your senior year when you see which colleges you have been accepted into. And at that point, I think it is prudent that you visit every college to which you have been accepted. But because the field is so competitive it may be that you have offers for between two and three schools at the end of the day. That would be an average number of acceptances and very good results. And at that time at the spring of your senior year you could go visit those colleges to which you have been accepted. So I would save my money and energy for those visits.

My collegeauditioncoach online prep membership has a comprehensive database of colleges and I have organized them in Reach, Fit and Safety categories based on the audition stats. I have also noted which are particularly strong in dance, academic rigor, and those who are known for having generous scholarship awards.

Your high school's college counselor should be able to help you compile your list although she or he may not have specific knowledge about theater and musical theater programs. You can still work together to start gathering lists of colleges. Your school counselor has some general knowledge that is helpful in terms of schools that would be a good academic fit for you (taking into consideration your GPA, SAT, and ACT scores) and nonaudition schools. You also want to keep your ears and eyes open for any friends who are performers and attending college BFA and BA programs in acting and musical theater. However, I want to caution you that a school that is a perfect fit for your best friend may not be the right school for you.

If you are in a financial position to hire an independent college counselor, I recommend Erin Ogren of Central Coast College Consultants. She has a special Performing Arts Package for acting and musical theatre applicants. Erin has advanced college-counseling accreditation and has been through the process with her own child recently, so she knows the ropes. I give her contact information under Resources.

Your public library is a free resource where you can find guidebooks that might be helpful. You can find many helpful reference books in bookstores. The Drama Book Shop in New York City is an excellent source for books about theatre and training. And Peterson's has a great online guide. They have a searchable database, School Of Visual And Performing Arts.

A free college-bound Internet community source is a Web site called *College Confidential*, also known as CC. CC has theater and musical theater chat rooms where laypersons, students, and family members who are going through the college audition process share advice, experiences, and opinions. However, to get accurate and up-to-date information, you always need to direct your inquiries to the individual colleges. I have listed these Web address under Resources at the end of the book.

If you like to network and want a free option for connecting to current college performing arts students, try Facebook. I have found Facebook extremely helpful with my private students. My current students friend my former students who are attending colleges and universities that are of interest to them. Many students (current and prospective) create groups where they can trade information about various performing arts programs. As Facebook friends, students can share information from firsthand experiences that they are not likely to get from college recruitment representatives. Often the best way to get personal and up-to-date information is to talk to a student who is currently enrolled in one of those programs that you are interested in. But I caution you again that what is best for one person may not be what is best for you, so keep that in mind.

It is important for you to keep an open mind and think about the specific things that you want in a college and the kind of training you need. Remember, these are your "Must-Haves". Do you want to live in a certain part of the country? Do you want a school that has strong academics? Do you want the full college experience with football, Greek life, and student government? Do you want a conservatory? Do you want to be close to home? Do you want to be far away from home? Is tuition going to be a make-or- break factor in your decision? What kinds of scholarships are available? These things are important considerations. Your college experience not only will be about your training in acting or musical theater but also will have a lasting impact on you in other ways. You may take up residence in the town where you go to college, make lifelong friends or meet the love of your life. You need to think about the kinds of people you want to go to school with and the environment in which you will be living. The college experience will enrich your life in ways beyond your training. These considerations are all part of the process.

Performing Arts Degrees

As you research college programs, you need to understand that there are different degrees and I am going to explain and define for you what the degrees are. I will also teach you about reach schools, fit schools and a safety schools. I want to explain what those terms mean and how to learn about the fit schools, especially, because you may not know about because they are not household names, but have excellent programs. The fit schools are the schools you will most likely get accepted into, so I want to talk to you about those. And you will see that there is a comprehensive list of colleges performing arts program at the back of my book. And I want to discuss how to compile smart lists with a good balance of reaches, fits and safeties.

It is important that you know what kind of degree you want. So let us explore the different degrees that are available for the study of acting and musical theater. The degrees that are going to be of greatest interest to you are a bachelor of arts (BA), a bachelor of fine arts, (BFA), and, to a lesser degree, a bachelor of music (BM). You could also consider a conservatory, which would include the BFA degree. A handful of training schools offer an eighteen-month or two-year associate of applied arts degree program (AA). KD Studio in Dallas, The Neighborhood Playhouse and Circle in The Square in New York City are examples. However, with the AA accreditation you will not graduate with a college degree, only a certificate.

BA, BFA, BM, Conservatory

A BA is a degree that is commonly defined as 30 percent to 40 percent curriculum in your major, with the remainder in general education and electives. If you want to double major or minor in something or maybe study abroad, a BA is an excellent degree plan for you. The BA is traditionally seen as a degree for people who have a wide variety of interests besides acting, singing, and dancing.

The BFA is defined as 60 percent to 80 percent curriculum in your major, with the remainder in general education and electives. The BFA leaves little room for a minor that is substantial, and it would be difficult to double major and still graduate in four years. The BFA curriculum is very intense and does not allow for time during the school year to study abroad; however, you could study abroad in the summer.

With the conservatory-styled BFA degree, expect 80 percent to 95 percent of the courses in your major and very little curriculum in general education. Your course selection is almost entirely related to your major with few or no classes outside your major. And, of course, the student body is going to be made up solely of students who are studying performing degrees. Some colleges, however, offer an intense conservatory style of training in a liberal arts university setting.

Lastly, a BM in musical theater is housed in the school of music and heavily weighted in music theory and classically based music repertoire such as sung through musicals and operettas. This is as opposed to post-1960-styled traditional acting, singing, and dancing musicals. These degrees are fewer in number.

Sometimes it is a good idea to have a mixture of degrees on your college list. But if you think of yourself as a performer first and want to train for the stage through a rigorous, challenging, demanding curriculum that is very performance driven, then head for a BFA. If you have a wide variety of interests and passions in addition to performing and want to explore those studies or want an abroad experience, take the BA route. Many excellent BA programs have a rigorous theater curriculum.

Frankly, directors are split on what kind of actors they like to hire. Some directors prefer actors who have a BA degree because they are well rounded in their education. For example, if you were cast in a production of *Les Miserables* and you had studied the French Revolution, French language, and history, you would make a larger contribution to the rehearsal process. You would bring more to the table, as they say. Whereas a BFA performer might have spent years studying dance, voice, and acting but have little knowledge about French history or French language. On the other hand, one school of thought says that the BFA-trained actor is ready to perform professionally because of the four years of intense performance training.

Whatever the degree, you need to do some real soul searching about what kind of education you want for yourself. Ask yourself these questions: Are your friends at school from other walks of life? Do you have friends who are athletes? Do you have friends who are involved in student government? Do you have friends who are cheerleaders? Or are all your friends actors, dancers, and musical theater types? Chances are if you are used to being around challenging academics and people who have a variety of interests and you go to a conservatory, you may feel like a fish out of water. You may find that your fellow conservatory students are nothing like you. Then again you may welcome that difference. These are all considerations that you need to discuss with your parents.

Reaches, Fits, and Safeties

You may have heard the term *reaches, fits, and safeties*. What does that mean? A *reach* is a school that has a very low acceptance rate (under 10 percent), is highly selective, and you dream of attending. A *fit* is a school that—considering your skill set, your type, and the school's acceptance rate—you will have a fairly good chance of being accepted into. You can get these statistics by contacting the program admissions office. A *safety* is a school that does not require an audition and one that you and your high school college counselor are certain you will get into based on your GPA, ACT, and SAT scores.

There are plenty of excellent nonaudition safeties for you to consider. Be sure your safeties have strong, reputable theater departments where you earnestly feel you could be happy if you are rejected from all your audition schools. No one wants to think about that scenario, but you must have a safety net, just in case.

A Smart List

I talk a lot with my students about creating a smart list. A smart list is a college list that includes a thoughtful combination of reaches, fits, and safeties. This is essential to your success. Creating a list of colleges is a long process, and your list will evolve over time. The important thing is for you to get the process started. Begin a dialogue with your parents. Begin a dialogue with the universities. Go to the college fairs. Talk to your college counselor. Talk to your performer friends who are already in college. Just get the process started, and do not expect that you are going to have all the answers right away. Know that this list of colleges is going to drive the rest of the process because each school has different audition requirements. And it is important for you to recognize your list as a first step in preparing for the rest of the process. Keep an open mind.

Students often ask how many schools should be on their list. The competition is stiff. You want to be able to have a couple of choices at the end of the day so that you feel as though you have some options. Having talent is not always enough to gain admittance. More often it is about type, not talent. Some colleges may already have someone your type, or they might be actively seeking a type different from yours. I tell this true story of a very talented female student whose type could be classified as brassy, belty, and brunette. She was rejected from her top choice school. When I asked the head of the department for feedback, he told me that she was the most talented girl they had auditioned that day, but they didn't need her type. The school was graduating three petite blonde legit sopranos, and their priority that audition year was to fill the holes in their department. Any other year she probably would have been accepted.

The most competitive category (in term of types auditioning) is the white female category. There are a disproportionately large number of white females auditioning for schools, so there is more competition within that group. For those I recommend a list of twelve to fifteen audition schools. If you are an ethnic minority or a male, ten-twelve audition schools should be enough. Remember, this does not include nonaudition safety schools. I recommend two safeties for everyone.

The makeup of your college list is more important than the number of schools. The list should ideally have more fits that reaches. And, *never more reaches than fits.* The list might include a combination of BAs, BFAs, maybe a BM or conservatory, plus the two nonaudition safeties.

Chapter Three
College Audition Requirements

Once you begin your college auditions during your senior year, you will learn that each school conducts their recruitment process differently. However, there are some aspects of the process that are generally true for most all schools. What I have done in this chapter is to outline the typical college audition requirements, so that you can begin to see what will be asked of you.

Requirements

Each audition has different components for acting and for musical theater. When the time comes for you to begin applying to schools, you must check with the individual colleges to find out their complete requirements. These can be found on the colleges' websites. Most acting programs require two monologues. Most musical theater programs will require one or two monologues and two songs. A dance combination will likely be a part of the musical theatre audition process and sometimes a music theory test is administered. A brief personal interview is a component of the audition for both acting and musical theatre.

Monologues

Most schools are going to require either one or two contemporary monologues. However, many colleges request one contemporary monologue and one classical monologue. This is especially true of straight acting programs. A contemporary monologue is a monologue written from 1900 to present day. A classical monologue is traditionally considered a monologue written before 1900. That would include the Greeks, Shakespeare, Moliere, Calderon and other pieces written in verse. Although contemporary monologues are written from 1900 to present day, I think it is important to pick monologues written in the last three to ten years.

You should steer clear of any accents or dialects when you are performing your college monologues. Because the auditors want to get to know who *you* are, it is a hindrance to hide behind a dialect or an accent. It is also important to choose material close to your own personality with an understanding of how you will be cast, and avoid extreme characters.

Hiring a monologue coach can be very be helpful and will provide guidance in finding monologues that are a right fit. To further assist you in finding appropriate material, some of the college websites will offer a list of recommended monologues (and a list of monologues to avoid).

Avoid monologues written specifically for monologue books. Your college audition monologues need to be from significant playwrights: either important young, contemporary writers or established well-known writers.

Go to the theatre and read plays. Expand your knowledge of plays, playwrights and composers.

Songs

For musical theatre auditions (and for a very few acting auditions), you will be required to sing two songs in addition to your one or two monologues. Acting programs that require you to sing usually accept one song of your choosing, sung a cappella. For musical theatre auditions, colleges want to hear an up-tempo and a ballad. Up-tempo is just that, an upbeat lively tune. A ballad is slower and contains a legato line or sustained vocal line. Even when schools do not require it, it is advisable to have one song that was written before 1960. And also a pop/rock song that could, but doesn't have to be from a musical. There are some schools (those more classically based, or offering a BM) that require an "art song" or classical song sung in a foreign language.

For musical theater programs, singing is the first and foremost component. Establishing your vocal identity is important. Choosing the correct song to showcase your vocal strengths for your castable type is extremely important. This is where a coach can be valuable. Acting the song is another crucial component for song preparation, and your college auditors look specifically for your understanding of this important component.

When colleges conduct off campus auditions, they may not provide live accompaniment. This will require that you prepare your music on recorded tracks. Simple recorded piano accompaniment is appropriate.

Sixteen and 32 bar cuttings are the standard requested from the schools. Additionally, you need to have your songbook ready. You "book" should contain other musical theatre and pop repertoire that you are familiar with in case the auditors ask you to sing additional material

Dance Combination

For musical theater college auditions, there is usually a required dance element. This will consist of a musical theater dance combination, typically four eight counts of music. A member of the faculty teaches the combo in a group setting. You will have approximately 15-30 minutes to learn the combination. This component is an important element of the audition requirement and is something you should be training for in the years and months leading up to the audition. You are going to have to be ready to execute ably whatever combination is thrown at you. Get in some dance classes now, if you are not already. I recommend ballet classes, three times a week.

Music Theory Test

Some musical theater auditions will ask you to take a music theory test. Sometimes this will be a test on a piece of paper, or a sight-reading exercise that you do with the accompanist and the auditor. Sometimes it will be a test that you take by playing the piano. It varies with each school but if there is a theory test, my suggestion would be for you to ask questions of the college before the audition about what kind of test it is and how it is going to be administered. Schools will be interested to know if you play a musical instrument and if you compose music. Usually the music theory test is used for placement and is not an admission qualifier. This is why taking piano now will benefit you.

Chapter Four

The Academic Component

Once you begin the application process senior year, you will follow the application requirements on the college websites. Because this book addresses what you need to be doing *before* that application process, I have enlisted the expertise of an independent college advisor. She will tell you what to do early in the process, so that you are ready when the time comes.

Your audition will count for as much as 80% in the admission decision for most BFA programs. But academics are also important, especially for scholarship money. I asked my colleague and college advisor, Erin Ogren, who specializes in performing arts applicants, to share her expertise about grades, course load, test prep, letters of recommendation and how it can affect scholarships/financial aid. Erin is an Independent College Consultant and works at a distance with students from around the U.S. and Canada. I encourage you to contact Erin, if you need the support of an independent college advisor. I have included her website in the Resources section in the back of this book.

Here are Erin's suggestions:

Get ready by asking yourself questions

Be attuned to what type of learner you are. Do you learn best by discussing, reading or listening? Are you a hands-on learner or do you prefer a more theoretical approach to learning? Are class discussions and relationships with your teachers important to you?

Consider that some colleges will allow you to double major or minor in another subject. What subjects in addition to acting or musical theater might be of interest to you, English literature or communications? Music composition? Arts management? Play writing? Be open to all the possibilities. High school is a time to explore. And it may be helpful to discover your personality type by taking an online assessment.

Grades

Academic performance matters too! At some colleges, like UCLA, they will not even evaluate your talent until you first meet specific academic thresholds. So do well in challenging high school core academic courses and increase your college options.

Course selection

Choose rigorous courses in areas of interest to you.

Academically, colleges want to see you challenge yourself rather than simply taking the easiest core course load available. Given the demands of your craft, time is a precious commodity so you needn't take every AP course available but do challenge yourself in those areas where you excel academically. Don't wait. At most colleges, sophomore and junior year academic performance matters most.

Academics and scholarships

Keep the doors open to many colleges by doing well in the classroom. Aside from offering need based financial aid, many colleges offer merit money to reward talent and academic achievement. In addition to offering "talent" money a department head may be able to entice you to attend their program with an academic scholarship if you are a stellar student.

IMPORTANT NOTE: Talk as a family about your financial situation early on in the process because it will color your selection of schools. Be realistic and frank about what you can afford.

Test Prep

All colleges will accept either the ACT or SAT. Do not go in cold. Prep sufficiently and do it early before taking these exams because many colleges will require the results of all exam sittings or dates.

Think hard about how you will best prep. Are you likely to tackle an online course or to work your way through a book on your own? Or perhaps you need a tutor working with you face to face in order to learn best and be held accountable.

Some academically selective schools also require individual SAT Subject Tests; take the exam right after completing the relevant course. If you take biology sophomore year, take the biology subject test spring of sophomore year while material is fresh in your mind rather than waiting until junior year when most students begin their test prep. Full on ACT and SAT prep need not begin until the summer before your junior year at the earliest.

For those students with test anxiety, a growing number of colleges are test optional and do not require either exam. Visit Fair Test, the national center for fair and open testing. I included their website in the Resources section.

Letters of Recommendation

Cultivate relationships with teachers you enjoy and your school counselor.   Many schools will want at least one academic teacher recommendation along with your school counselor's recommendation.   Let them know you are college bound and care about both your academic and onstage performance.   Most colleges will require a recommendation from someone who has worked with you in the performing arts realm as well.

Volunteer Work

Your time should be spent primarily on the stage so tie volunteer work to your craft. Giving feels good. Mentor along younger students by volunteering for local youth theater, vocal or instrumental groups or perform in productions touring local elementary schools. Help local groups raise funds through performances at "Sing for your Supper" type events. These types of volunteer work are far more meaningful than running out sporadically to volunteer in areas unrelated to the arts. Unless of course you have a developing or ongoing interest in another area that you may want to pursue in college as well.

Chapter Five

Mock Auditions and Master Classes

Many of my seniors and their parents tell me they feel they should have started participating in mock auditions and master classes much earlier than senior year. So I've decided to present information for you in this chapter about mock auditions and why you might find them advantageous to participate in as a freshman or sophomore.

In order to find where these master classes and mock auditions are you can go to my website store page at collegeauditioncoach.com. I have a wonderful selection of master classes and mock auditions that take place on the various college campuses throughout the country and there are also classes that exist through other sources You can simply find those on the internet, if you begin searching.

Once you have prepared audition material, have it memorized and rehearsed, you need to get "audition ready". Over the years I have learned that the best way to prepare my students for their actual performance is through a series of master classes (or mock auditions).

You can begin participating in these classes as soon as you feel ready. This should begin *before* senior year. Freshmen and sophomores regularly take part. Obviously, if you are a freshman or sophomore, you probably won't have your final college audition presentation finalized. But you can bring preliminary songs and monologue material into the master classes to begin working on perfecting your presentation. That way, when the time comes, you will have a good sense of what a college audition will be like and how to prepare for it.

What exactly is a master class or mock audition? This is a small class, usually ten-fifteen students with one college professor or master teacher. My master classes are styled to resemble a real college audition, except that I allow parents to observe. Students perform their audition material, songs and/or monologues and get feedback from the master teacher. All this is to show exactly what the college audition is going to look and feel like, and also provide feedback on audition material from the professors who actually conduct auditions for college admissions. Another benefit is that it takes the mystery out of the process and begins to build confidence. Students get to watch each other perform audition material and listen to the feedback from the master teacher. In addition, the class is a wonderful opportunity for students to network early on with some of the colleges and begin to build personal relationships with the professors and the people who will be auditioning you when the time comes for your real college auditions. And many of your fellow student performers in the class are from other parts of the country. By attending these master classes, you are beginning to lay the foundation for a nation-wide community of like-minded young thespians. These are the same individuals you will encounter as you go through the audition process. Thus, establishing a lot of familiar faces. These master classes are not just for songs and monologues. Classes often include a mock dance audition for musical theatre hopefuls. Usually, the teacher will rework the performance, make adjustments and give written or oral feedback.

As I said earlier, in my master classes, I allow parents to observe. And if younger teens are not ready to participate, they are also welcome to observe or audit the classes. This is done frequently. Students and parents can learn much from watching the master teacher work with the other students in the class. Most of my parents say it is a real eye opener. I conduct these throughout the year in various cities around the country and on campuses with experienced college auditors. A current listing of master classes can be found on my website Store page at collegeauditioncoach.com.

It is important that you feel confident in your material and that you feel relaxed, comfortable and ready to perform when the real audition day comes. If participating in one of my mock auditions and master classes is not possible, you can ask your high school drama teacher or choir teacher to allow you to rehearse your pieces in a mock setting in a classroom. If that is not going to be an option for you, perform your audition for your family and friends whenever possible.

Because students watch each other perform and listen to the auditor's oral critiques, they learn a great deal. And hearing different critiques is also a good reminder that there will be as many different opinions of your audition as there are colleges. This further emphasizes how subjective the audition process is. My on-campus master classes include a tour, which is particularly informative. As I said, the classes are also a wonderful way to begin networking with the college reps. It is a good idea to start participating in these mocks as soon as you have monologue and song material performance ready. Participate in as many master classes and mocks as possible, or simply observe. It will build your confidence better than anything I know.

Chapter Six

Performance Resume
and Headshot

Your Resume

Your resume is primarily a representation of your performance credits and may include experience in related fields. As a freshman or sophomore, you are still building your resume and gaining credits. Be sure to keep it updated and current. You will present your performance resume (stapled to your headshot) to the auditors at all your auditions. A performance resume should be only one page.

Here is an example of what I consider to be a well-prepared college audition resume.

STUDENT NAME

E-mail and cell phone

Eyes: Blue, Hair: Red, Weight 120, Height: 5' 5 1/2"

SCHOOL PRODUCTIONS

The Crucible	Mary Warren	The Hockaday School
La Casa de Bernarda Alba	Bernarda Alba*	The Hockaday School
The Real Inspector Hound	Moon*	The Hockaday School
And Then They Came for Me	Eva Geringer*	Dallas Children's Theater
Metamorphoses	Various	The Hockaday School
The Giver	Fiona	Dallas Children's Theater
Street Scene	Alice Simpson	The Hockaday School
The Sound of Music	Gretl	The Hockaday School
After Juliet	Bianca	The Hockaday School
The Miracle Worker	Helen Keller*	Dallas Children's Theater
The Secret Garden	Mary Lennox*	Dallas Children's Theater
The Music Man	Winthrop	The Hockaday School
To Kill a Mockingbird	Scout*	Dallas Children's Theater
Sarah, Plain and Tall	Rose	Dallas Children's Theater
The Island of the Skog	Skog	Dallas Children's Theater

TRAINING

VOICE Brian Schexnayder, 3 years; DANCE former company member,
The Centre For Dance, and Power House of Dance, 5 years

HONORS

Interlochen Fine Arts Award; International Thespian Society; National Shakespeare Competition
2nd place; Presidential Scholar in the Arts Honorable Mention Award

Be sure your resume is well organized and easy to read. A standard sheet of paper is slightly larger than an 8X10 headshot so you will need to trim the resume to fit your 8X10 picture. And staple it (facing out) to the back of your headshot. I suggest an inset thumbnail of your headshot as shown in the example. This makes it easy for the auditors to see your face while they view your resume, without having to flip the page over to see your headshot. And use a colored font. A black and white resume seems a bit old fashioned.

Your Headshot

All actors need a headshot. It is how the agents, casting directors and college auditors remember you. But at this early stage for you, I wouldn't spend a lot of money on an expensive headshot. Using a professional photographer can cost from four to six hundred dollars. At your age, just a snapshot of your face and shoulders that is current and looks like you is going to be adequate. Be sure it is well lit and you look happy and friendly. I have provided examples of what a good professional headshot looks like, and that is something you might want to consider later. But you are still young and your looks are going to be changing a lot, so don't invest in an expensive headshot right now. Just be sure that you have a current snapshot of yourself for any auditions that might come your way. You could just take a selfie, or have a friend take it. Or you may have a school photo that will be just fine. Print your headshot in 8X10 size and have your name printed at the bottom. And be sure that you staple your headshot to your one page performance resume when you go to auditions, or when you apply to summer programs.

Here are examples of excellent professional headshots. These are taken by the fabulous Kelsey Edwards. Her website is listed in the Resources section. Your headshot should be exactly that, a picture of your face and shoulders. Be sure that your headshot is pleasant and welcoming and looks like you.

As I said, for your early high school years, it is not necessary to have a professional headshot. And when you are auditioning for colleges during your senior year, you can use your senior picture, if getting a professional headshot is not in your budget. However, an excellent professional headshot is an important investment because it serves as your calling card every time you have an audition.

Wardrobe

The wardrobe choice for your audition and headshot is a reflection of your individual personality and marketable type. It is important that you look like you put some effort into your choice of attire, but I recommend that your clothes be simple.

If you are not sure about your own personal style, play it safe and follow these guidelines. For girls, I prefer a casual dress in a color that is complimentary and well fitted. In your headshot, only the top will be seen. Try different colors and necklines. Avoid prints, stripes or patterns that will be distracting. Guys should wear khakis or corduroys with a shirt tucked in with a belt. And your shirt can be a solid color or a sweater that is flattering. You should look pressed, clean and fresh when you walk in the room. You can wear the same thing in your headshot and for your auditions, if you want. Be sure you practice your audition in the clothes you plan on wearing, including shoes. And shoes should be practical and comfortable.

Chapter Seven

Audition Locations

In planning ahead for your college auditions, you will have several options. You can begin thinking about the different audition environments now and talking with your family about which ones make sense for you. It is likely that you will need to participate in some combination of the ones listed below, as your list of colleges will generally dictate your audition locations.

On-Campus Auditions

Some schools hold auditions only on campus. The schools' Web site gives you their dates and times. Other schools have auditions on campus as well as regional off-campus auditions. Although auditioning on campus gives the college recruitment office a chance to impress you, it does not increase your chances of being admitted to the school. It does give you a firsthand look at the campus and the surrounding area. Some colleges offer complimentary tickets to see a school show if there is a performance at the time of your audition.

Off-Campus Auditions

Many schools participate in off-campus regional auditions in various cities throughout the United States. These usually begin in early fall, and some colleges continue their audition tour until late February. You will need to check the schools' Web sites to see if they are conducting auditions in a city near you. These regional auditions are often held in a hotel conference room. This can be a great convenience and money saver for your family. The National Unified Auditions are the largest regional auditions. I have shared detailed information about Unifieds later in this chapter.

Consortium Auditions

Regional consortium auditions happen around the country. Some are on the West Coast, some are in the South, and some are in the Midwest. College representatives and auditors attend the International Thespian Convention, various state thespian conventions, the North Texas Drama Auditions, and a variety of consortium auditions around the country. These consortiums are group auditions, with twenty to fifty colleges in attendance. The college representatives are all in one room at the same time, usually a theater or convention hall. The students come in one at a time and perform their audition for all the auditors simultaneously. Most of the students have not yet applied to the colleges in attendance. Typically, the audition is ninety seconds long and strictly timed. Most students perform two monologues (for straight acting programs) or a brief monologue and forty to forty-five seconds of a song (for musical theater). When all the auditions are over, there is a callback. During the callback, no additional performance is asked of the student. The college that has called students back will encourage them to apply to their school and answer any questions you have about their program. The auditors might want to see the students in a more extended audition setting, such as their campus or one of their regional auditions, to perform additional songs or monologues. They may need to see students dance or have additional faculty members meet them. In some rare cases the auditors will actually offer an artistic acceptance on the spot for acting, musical theater, or vocal performance programs during the call back. This really depends on the recruitment style of the individual college.

National Unified Auditions

Three different college theater educators from three different universities got together some years back and cofounded the National Unified Auditions to accommodate large numbers of students who are auditioning for multiple colleges. Those pioneer gentlemen were, and still are, Charley Helfert from Southern Methodist University, Peter Sargeant from Webster University, and John David Lutz from the University of Evansville.

Universities that are National Unified member schools and offer undergraduate degrees in acting and musical theater programs convene in the same city on the same dates and hold their auditions. Each individual college holds its auditions separately in a hotel meeting room or at nearby locations or studios. Unlike the consortium concept, where all the auditors from all the colleges are in the same room, the National Unified Auditions are held separately and privately by each member school. These auditions begin in late January and continue until late-February.

At the time of this writing, there are twenty-five National Unified member colleges, universities, and conservatories. Auditors from these schools travel to New York for two days, Chicago for three days, and Los Angeles for two days, and Las Vegas for two days. When you apply for admission and schedule your audition for a Unified member school, you may choose an off-campus Unified Audition site for convenience. Simply pick the city (New York, Chicago, Los Angeles, or Las Vegas) in which you want to schedule your audition. The individual colleges have these locations and dates listed on their Web sites.

Auditioning through the Unified system has many benefits: it saves you money and time auditioning a number of times while having to travel to only one city. I prefer the Chicago and Los Angeles sites for several reasons. Most of the colleges hold their auditions at the same hotel. You simply go down the elevator to the appropriate meeting room, assuming that you are staying in the hotel. It is very easy and stress free. Chicago is the only site where the Unified schools hold auditions for three days. The other cities have only two days of auditions. I will say that the warm weather in L.A. is a nice plus and the atmosphere is more laid back.

Every year I attend the Unified Auditions in Chicago and Los Angeles with my students and have been doing do since 2005. I feel it is a very effective method for auditioning for multiple schools.

Prescreen Audition

Because of the increased number of applicants, some of the more popular schools have begun prescreening candidates. It is a very smart way, I think, for colleges to narrow down the list of auditionees to those most likely to be a good fit for their university. In these cases, the colleges request an electronic or live prescreen submission prior to granting an in-person audition. You will shoot these in September-October as you apply to the college programs, as I mentioned in the College Audition Timeline in Chapter Two. Artistic prescreens usually take the form of an electronic submission that you upload to a third party applicant and management online service. Your submission can be something simple that you record at home, or you could hire a professional videographer. Complete guidelines are available on the college websites. I have an excellent instructional video on shooting your prescreens. It is available on my website Store page at collegeauditioncoach.com.

Digital Audition

If you are unable to get to the campus for an audition, a growing number of colleges allow you to do your complete college audition via an electronic submission. This is not the same as the prescreen. It simply takes the place of an in-person audition. I expect a trend toward more colleges accepting digital audition submissions as the applicant pool continues to increase. As of this writing, New York University's Tisch School of the Arts accepts a digital audition submitted as an e-mail attachment and a live interview over the Internet via Skype. This may seem an unusual venue for an audition, but I have been interacting with students all over the country via Skype and FaceTime for years with great success. I have also preliminarily introduced some of my students to college auditors using their YouTube performances. The Internet provides a form of online communication that we are becoming accustomed to. When an in-person audition and interview are not possible, a digital submission provides a viable alternative.

Chapter Eight

Mental Preparation

In this chapter, I have included advice from two mental health professionals who have specific experience counseling young performers. It is imperative that students maintain a positive mental attitude and develop tools for handling rejection. You will get more rejections that you will acceptances. Also, parents need advice in advance of the college audition process on how to offer support without smothering, and finding the line for healthy boundaries.

Bill Crawford, Ph.D. and owner of Crawford Performance Solutions, is a psychologist, author and speaker to many BFA performing arts college programs. In addition, he is a parent of two young artists. His new book, "*Freeing the Artistic Mind*" gives performing and visual artists new information on how to minimize their anxiety, and maximize their confidence and creativity by accessing a specific part of the brain. You can learn more about his work at www. BillCrawfordPhD.com.

Heather Sumlin is the Director of Performance Programs at Mental Management® Systems. Heather has been coaching for ten years focusing on helping performers reach their potential under pressure. Mental Management® Systems was founded by Olympic Champion, Lanny Bassham in 1977 and is used by performers and competitors across the globe. The book "With Winning in Mind" is the best first step to understanding and implementing what they teach. www. mentalmanagement.com

FOR PARENTS

I asked Bill to contribute advice for parents, and here is what he said.

We've all heard the stories… stage parents who are living vicariously through their children…helicopter parents who won't let their children do anything on their own… parents who act like managers and seem to think that they must intimidate everyone they meet so that their little star gets the best treatment, etc., and what comes at the end of each of these stories is the negative effect these types of parents had on their children.

As the parent of a young artist myself (my son is in a competitive BFA Acting program), I know how tempting it can be to want to be involved in our children's lives.   So, what is the answer? Do we just drop them off at the theater (or theater school) and hope for the best? No! The truth is that our kids need our love and support, and we can and should play a vital role in their growing up to be happy, healthy, confident adults.

To do this however, we need to know how to be supportive without smothering, how to give advice without sending the message that we have no confidence in their ability to figure things out on their own, how to help them deal with the unpredictable world of a performing artist without becoming their "manager," and most importantly, how to lay a foundation for the adult-to-adult relationship we want when they are on their own.

For example:

1. *Advice*: The problem with giving our kids advice when they haven't asked for it is that often they take it as an insult… as if we have no confidence in what they know, or their ability to make good decisions.

The Solution: Be clear about your intent, and give them the opportunity to tell you what they know first. You might say something like,

"Honey, I want to be sure you are safe at this party, however, I don't want to tell you what you already know, so could you tell me what you plan to do to stay safe so that I can feel good about your going?" Then fill in any blanks. Also, let them teach you something and/or give you advice as often as possible.

2. *Support*: They need to know that we believe in their talent... but don't expect that to be enough. Why? Because they think that we are SUPPOSED to love them and see them as wonderful. Therefore, they don't see our evaluation as something that will get them "chosen" by others. It is necessary *("I mean, if my own parents don't think I'm any good, what chance to I have?")* but they can't rely on it to predict their success. Therefore, don't take it as rejection when they seem to minimize your praise.

3. *Failure*: When our kids are not chosen for a part or a program, they are not looking to feel better, at least not right away. First they need to grieve a bit of a shattered dream. Their sadness is an indication of how much they care. What they really may need is a safe place to grieve, and someone who isn't going to minimize their pain. Then, when they are ready, tell them how much you love them, and how confident you are in their talent. Take them back to a time when they were totally immersed in a performance, and remind them of what that felt like. This feeling (and hard work, of course) will be the key to their success in the future.

4. *Your Relationship*: This is most important because it will last for the rest of your lives. The thing to remember is that every time you are interacting with your child you are co-creating your relationship. Your goal should be to create a relationship that supports their success

now and in the future, and one that allows them to stay connected to you when they become an adult. Ask yourself the question, "What are the qualities and characteristics I want my young artist to have when he or she becomes an adult? Respectful? Loving? Self-confident? Compassionate? Considerate? If so, then this is how you treat them. Kids learn what they live, and how their parents see them will become part of who they are, and stay with them for the rest of their lives.

FOR STUDENTS

I asked Heather to share advice for students. Here is what she writes.

Mental preparation is performer specific. Not every performer will approach auditions the exact same way mentally but there are some things all performers should understand in order to have a better chance of performing at their best. First, the environment should not control or dictate your thought process. The environment will always give us something to think about but that doesn't mean we should focus on it. For example, there may be other people waiting to audition talking about their successes or their fears. Your parents, friends or strangers can pull your focus by talking to you, texting you or calling you right before your audition. There are hundreds of possibilities of things the environment can give you that will be tempting to focus on. From not feeling well, to overhearing someone else audition who is amazing, to butterflies that seem to take over your tummy. You absolutely need to be in control of your thoughts before an audition and not allow the distractions to pull your focus. You have spent a tremendous amount of time preparing technically for this incredible opportunity don't allow others or circumstances to affect your ability to be successful.

At Mental Management® Systems we teach our students how to prepare mentally in practice as well as on competition day by helping them learn how to control their minds under pressure. There are helpful and harmful ways of thinking. Be sure to focus on something helpful before an audition. For example, worrying about the audition is harmful, believing you will do great and trusting your training is helpful. Make sure your thoughts moments before the audition are decided in advance. Prepare those thoughts so you can duplicate them when it matters. You will spend months memorizing the lines of your monologue and deciding on the character, blocking, etc. in order to be able to trust that you can deliver the best performance. Your mental approach should also be decided and certain. How do you want to feel in your audition? What do you want the auditors to believe about you? Focus on things that make the possibility of your audition being a success more likely. Focus on things you can control. You cannot control what other people do, say or think. Whether you are selected for the part is also outside of your control. Spending time focusing on whether or not your will get the part is a waste of precious time and also adds unneeded pressure to you. Your thought process before you audition should be connected to something that helps you trust your training, puts you in a calm mindset and it should be something you can repeat it every time you audition.

The next thing a performer should understand is the importance of building their Self-Image regarding their audition and their ability to perform under pressure. Without a strong Self-Image a performer is less likely to perform up to their potential. Think about it this way, if we are playing tennis and I think you can beat me and you think you can beat me, it's over for me. My Self-Image says, "It's like me to lose the tennis match". Is it like you to have a strong audition? It should be if you have trained well but you may have to adjust your Self-Image to make that statement a reality. Your thoughts control your Self-Image growth depending on the quality of those thoughts.

If you think negatively about your performance your Self-Image shrinks, if you think positively it grows. You need to be mindful that your job as a performer is not only to build your skill through practice, master classes, private coaching, and performances but your job is also to protect and build your own Self-Image as a performer by controlling your thoughts regarding your skill.

The world of performance that you have chosen to enter is full of exciting and powerful successes but also tremendous disappointment and rejection. Every audition has the possibility of being a giant leap toward success or a set back. Handling rejection is vital to your ability to have longevity in this career field. My father, Olympic Medalist, Lanny Bassham, says, "Adversity is the currency of champions." This basically means that those who succeed in life have to learn how to overcome before they can become who they strive to be. You will not land every role you audition for or get into every school your apply for and this is good thing. If we always succeeded the thrill of victory would be lost. The reason success is so incredible is because it is rare. Look at every outcome as positive and every audition as practice. You are a student of your craft, constantly learning, and constantly growing. Keep your mind focused on what you love about performing, focus on the things you can control and be mindful to always grow your Self-Image through positive thoughts, words and actions.

And Heather has one final comment for parents:

Parents of performers have an incredible responsibility to help build the Self-Image of their young performers. You are the first mental coach your child will have and your main objective should be to make sure to speak to your teen in a way that helps to grow their Self-Image. You are their safe place, the one who comforts them, protects them and builds them. Their Self-Image needs to be built and you have the ability to help in this process by focusing on their successes, listening to them and giving them helpful guidance that allows them to see themselves in the best light possible and supporting their dreams and goals.

Chapter Nine

College Acceptances

Because you are not applying to colleges right now, I won't go into too much excruciating detail with this, but you can get much more information in my book, I GOT IN! And please note that my expertise is in the area of college audition admission. The academic evaluation as it applies to college admissions should be attained from a bona fide college counselor.

I will tell you generally that when you have completed an audition for college programs you won't get any feedback at all most likely, and you certainly won't know if you have gotten in the program until later when you get an official response. Some schools offer rolling admission, which means they send out acceptances as they audition throughout the recruitment season. Students typically are notified about two weeks to one month after the audition. Other schools will not make any offers of acceptance until March or even as late as April 1. So there is a lot of waiting that takes place after your auditions, and you just have to learn to be patient and understand that the long wait time is all part of the process. Some schools have dual admission, meaning you have to be accepted into the university academically in conjunction with being accepted artistically into the program to which you have applied and auditioned for. Other schools admission is bifurcated. It could be that you get accepted academically to a university but do not get accepted into the program at that university. So every school is different, and you will learn about that as you go through the application process. It is one of the things that families find most confusing and most complex because there is no uniformity in the way the colleges conduct recruitment or conduct their admission process. Again, an experienced college audition coach or college counselor can really be an asset during this time.

Acceptances

Schools with rolling admission will offer acceptances usually 2-3 weeks after your audition. Schools without rolling admissions will notify you of their decision in March or April.

Most acceptances will come via snail mail. However, some schools send initial emails, and some of the smaller programs like to make personal phone calls to deliver the good news. Most often they will call the student directly on his or her cell phone. A complete acceptance package will eventually arrive in the mail. Information on financial aid packages may be included in the initial mailing, but some scholarship awards may arrive in subsequent mailings. Each school is different.

Rejections

Formal rejections almost always come in the form of snail mail. These form letters are cordial and brief. You will not be given any specific reason for the rejection or any audition feedback. I do know of some specific occasions where a more personal email was sent, but that is unusual and entirely up to the discretion of the theatre admissions personnel and individual auditors.

Deferrals/Waitlists

Deferrals and waitlist notifications usually come in the form of emails and letters.

A deferral means that a college is deferring their decision until all (or some portion) of their auditions are over. So they have neither rejected or accepted you, but are placing you in the pool of applicants under consideration.

A waitlist means that a decision was made not to initially accept you. However, remaining on the waitlist gives you the opportunity to be accepted at a later date if the school chooses to go to its waitlist in the event that it does not fill all its slots with first round offers. Some waitlists are ranked. Some are by type. Some are divided by male and female. It depends on the school.

One important piece of advice: if you are waitlisted or deferred by a school that you have a strong interest in, be sure you stay in touch with them regularly. Show that you are interested by updating them on any performances, improved test scores, awards and honors you might receive, or just a thank you note. This would also be an excellent time to visit the campus.

Accepting an Offer

The national "reply by" date is May 1^s. Any offer made to you stands until you have responded by May 1. A request in writing for an extension may be granted if you need additional time to make your decision. Schools would certainly like to get an answer from you as soon as possible after the offer is made, (especially if they have rolling admissions) but you have no obligation to do so. You have until May 1st to make you final decision.

And I do stress to my students, as a courtesy to others, please notify a school immediately if you have decided not to attend.

After You Receive Your Admission Decisions:

You must notify each college or university that accepts you whether you are accepting or rejecting its offer. You should make these notifications as soon as you have made a final decision as to the college that you wish to attend, but no later than May 1. It is understood that May 1 will be the postmark date. You may confirm your intention to enroll and, if required, submit a deposit to only one college or university.

Chapter Ten

College Audition Coaching

Many people tell me that they didn't even know there was such a thing as a coach for college auditions. College audition coaching is relatively new to the admission process. I started coaching for college auditions in the year 2000, and I was the first person doing that full time. Since then, many college audition coaches have popped throughout the country. So if you do decide you want a coach, you won't have any trouble finding one if you use the Internet to research, or talk to friends or other people who have been through the process.

You will find that there are different opinions about whether hiring a college audition coach is really necessary. What exactly does a college audition coach do? I can tell you what I do as a coach, and any experienced coach will probably offer similar services.

I think of myself as an advocate for my students and families and what I do is guide them through the process, help them navigate this complex intricate web of college performing arts applications and auditions. I help find the programs and the schools that are going to give them what they want and need. I help them find their audition material, monologues and songs, if that is applicable. I help them learn about how to define their type and how to know who they are and then show who they are in the audition room. I help them with scholarships and financial aid and I help ready them to be the best they can be, and build their confidence so that they go into the college audition process with joy and a feeling of high self esteem. The College Audition Coach motto is: Be Joyous, because you love this; Be Brave, because you are fierce; Be Yourself, because you are enough.

Coaches are not cheap. But many families feel they are well worth the money. Parents might not blink at spending $1000 for SAT prep. So, when the audition counts for as much as 80% in the admission process, why not spend your money on the audition prep? Expect to pay a coach $75 to $200 an hour. I would recommend that you find someone who is very experienced in the specific college audition process. Many voice teachers and acting teachers and performance coaches are very good at what they do. However, if they don't have the specific knowledge of the college audition process, I think you will find that they are not going to be adequate to lead you. College auditioning is very specialized. If you decide to get help in the process be sure that you hire someone who is a bona fide college audition coach with many years of experience. Check on their references and see that they have had good results in the past getting their kids into performing arts college programs.

I do know that there are many talented students who have success in the college audition process without any kind of coaching. So I would not say that it is a necessity. But I do feel as though it is very helpful and can ease a lot of tension between parents and students. A coach can actually save you money and heartache in the end, if you have been thoughtful in the way you approach the process and been well prepared, and in turn yielded nice offers.

Again, although it is not mandatory that you hire a coach, it can be extremely worthwhile, as you will learn from former parents in the section, *If I Knew Then, What I Know Now*. The audition process is complicated and stressful. Many families swear that having someone by their side, who is familiar with the experience, is a lifesaver.

My Coaching

When I coach a student, I am also guiding the family as a whole. First we participate in an online consultation when we get to know one another and discuss the "Must-Haves". These are the things that the student and parents want in the program, and in the university. Some examples of must-haves include: size and location, ability to perform in both plays and musical, academic rigor, the degree BA or BFA and available scholarships.

Once we establish the most important must-haves, we build the college list. I have a database of college performing arts programs that is a part of the online prep membership. I have categorized my list of colleges in categories of Reach, Fit and Safety. I also have special keys icons to denote programs particularly strong in dance, or have a high academic standard and those who have lower tuition or are known for generous scholarships. Another important consideration when building the list is that it is a good balance, and not top heavy in reach schools, as I mentioned in chapter three. Once we have a working list of colleges, I learn more about the student's personality through the Know My Type assessment. This is a fun online quiz that my students complete, along with input from family, friends and teachers. Coaching begins with my search for the perfect monologue material that fits the student's personality and is age appropriate and within their life experience. I have over seven hundred and fifty monologues, so the Know My Type data helps lead me to the monologue material that best fits the student's personality. If songs are needed, my team of song coaches get to work on searching for the perfect repertoire to show off the student's vocal strengths. Dance assessment is also a part of the prep. Once coaching is complete, I recommend participating in one of my master classes, as I discussed in chapter five.

Throughout the audition season, I make myself available via email, text, phone and video conferencing for consulting and coaching. I attend the National Unified auditions with my students, as well and host my own private auditions in Dallas in November with approximately twenty colleges in attendance. After all auditions have been completed, I get back together with my families in a follow-up online consult to discuss offers and scholarships before families make their final decisions. I always leave the final decision up to my families and students.

Coaching students and guiding families is my bliss. We become very close. I am not just their coach. I am their advocate, mentor, best friend, teacher, therapist and adopted mother. My work gives me more reward each and every year. But nothing gives me more happiness that when they call and say, "I got in!" That is the greatest reward of all.

Conclusion

I hope this primer has given you useful information as you contemplate the college audition process.

Your child's passion for acting or musical theater is an important expression of his or her inner creative spirit. Let that spirit soar and your child will make wonderful personal discoveries, build confidence and forge lasting friendships with like-minded teens.

If you feel certain that further study in the performing arts at the college level is part of your family's plan, stay the course and pursue the best training possible. Check out my book, *I GOT IN! The Ultimate College Audition Guide For Acting And Musical Theatre*, when the time comes. You will find it to be extremely helpful.

If you are interested in coaching, let me hear from you. Please visit my website at, collegeauditioncoach.com.

Break a leg! And remember: Be Joyous, Be Brave, Be Yourself.

If I Knew Then,
What I Know Now

Included is advice from parents who have been through the college audition process. I asked what they would do differently if they had the chance to do things over again, and also to share what they did right.

General Advice

Read a lot of plays. Classical works. New works. Get a feel for dialogue and pacing. Know the famous playwrights. Don't just read monologues – you need full context, so go find the whole play and READ it. Your local library is a great place to start!

Get to know YOU – A few years from now, when you audition for school, you need to pick material that suits YOU. If your style is more indie than preppy, you'll need to find age-appropriate monologues and/or songs that suit your unique flair. As you read plays, think about which characters you identify with and which roles you could play and why.

Get help – talk to your drama teachers and youth/community theatre directors about your interest in an acting career. Networking is an important skill to learn at a young age and they may suggest classes to take or other professional resources that can help you.

Use your summers wisely – sign up for one of the fabulous performing arts camps, If you need a scholarship to attend these camps, start researching requirements now.

Compete – Enter the national Young Arts awards or any of the regional performing arts competitions in your area. These are all great things to have on your arts resume and provide excellent experience.

Start early! These kids (especially girls) have to cast a wide net when these programs take so few kids.

Keep up your grades. It is a lot for a performing arts kid to juggle a rigorous course load with rehearsals and lessons and other activities. But having a high GPA and strong test scores can pay off in terms of academic merit scholarships when you apply to college. Talk to your guidance counselor about the best high school classes for you to take.

Start with a real understanding of what you can/will afford to spend towards college and a realistic understanding of where you stand in terms of financial aid.

If you want to get college audition experience as a junior you may want to consider going to Southeastern Theatre Conference (SETC). There are workshops and a college fair.

Many state Thespian conventions have auditions with college recruiters.

The single most important thing you can do Freshman and Sophomore year is to attend the National Association For College Admissions Counseling (NACAC) Performing and Visual Arts College Fair. It travels to many cities nationwide.

I think its a good thing for parents to start researching schools as soon as they realize their students are serious about majoring in theatre in college

Caution your kid to not fall in love with a school prematurely.

Consider hiring a coach. If I could go back to my daughter's junior year, I definitely would've sprung for private coaching. Some kids are very successful without one, but I really do think that the money spent would've been a great investment

Get your ACT/SAT out of the way as early as possible so you aren't stressing about it senior year or, if you wish to improve your score, you have plenty of time to study and re-take it.

If possible, do not have your child be in a show during the spring of her senior year. After the acceptances come in, you well may need/want to visit the programs again and this can be tough if you are in rehearsals or shows

Don't visit campuses unless your child has been accepted there. Or unless, they plan on auditioning on campus. It's a lot of money, and the chances are against them that they'll be accepted at some of these top schools. Best to get in first, and then make the rounds to see what environment they feel most comfortable in.

Instead of listening to folks around you or reading people's opinions online, sit down and find out WHAT is it exactly your child wants, what are THEY interested in, what is it that THEY need to become better performers/people, and then try to find the schools that could complete that puzzle for them.

It is important is to know, to REALLY know what the school costs, plus living expenses, books, etc. so you know what is a possibility for your family and what is NOT.

Most important thing I did was hiring an audition coach. The assistance we got with details, organization, deadlines, etc. was a huge benefit and well worth the cost. We were given a load of information on schools and their particular strengths and weaknesses, which helped us figure out what would be a better fit for our son.

For those specifically interested in musical theatre

Ballet! If you take no other dance classes, take ballet. It is the foundation of all dance training.

Take voice lessons with a teacher trained in musical theatre styles and teaching proper singing technique. (As opposed to just pop/rock/classical styles.) Contact your local music teachers' association or college music department for recommendations.

Keep up your instrumental music lessons if you already take them, or take basic piano lessons if you don't. Most musical theatre programs require music theory and keyboard skills, so you can get a head start in your training.

If we knew then what we know now, we would have started the process earlier than junior year.

We would have also exposed our daughter to more dance and singing lessons, and regional theater.

Make sure your child does really well in school academically. That will put him/her in good position to get a lot more scholarship money for school than her musical theatre talent will.

Attend summer intensives sophomore year.

If your kid isn't a dancer, START NOW. Actually, that's not soon enough: start yesterday!

Our son did high school theatre. He was unhappy in the program and did not get the roles, opportunities or recognition he had hoped for. But he had terrific experiences in several community theaters. When his younger sister started performing, she pursued her training through community theatre, rather than high school. In the end, it didn't seem to matter where they had experience and training as long as they had it. Both got into several fine schools and chose to study BFA Musical Theater at one of the most select programs.

Take piano!

Attend a summer program at a school that offers a musical theatre BFA. It is a great opportunity for training and learning. It also can give you a sense of whether this is really what you want to do in college. Finally, it gives you an opportunity to work with other talented students from around the country and can give you perspective of how you fit into the mix

The coaching investment was well worth it. We would not have selected the right songs. And monologues, we would have overlooked programs that we ended up really liking

Take more dance classes.

Focus on grades. PSAT/ACT prep early

Start researching the musical theatre programs, and even visiting schools that happen to be nearby.

Get a coach of some kind, or at least someone who can really help with monologue and song choices

Have your student start learning about the breadth and depth of the Broadway Canon now.

The hunt for the right repertoire is agonizing if you don't have a strong background in the genre. Hiring a coach to help pick songs can, of course, save a lot of time.

We started early and I'm glad we did. Sometimes I wish we had started earlier!

Have your child experience a bigger talent pool (in a summer experience) than what is available locally.

Attending Master Classes with college professors as a sophomore gave our son an early introduction to the top college programs.

One of the biggest mistakes that can be made is to limit your schools to those that have a "reputation" of being a "top school". If you limit your applications to only the "top" schools and avoid those that are excellent but inaccurately and broadly brushed with the misnomer of "second tier", your odds of disappointment at the end of the process are greatly increased.

If at all possible, use an experienced vocal coach/teacher to assist you in preparing songs for your auditions.

Parents, resist the compulsion to become hyper-invested in this process. Your kids will need you as their "safe harbors" to come to when they are emotionally or physically exhausted. Help them to maintain their sense of balance, perspective and optimism and to recharge their batteries.

Determine your "type", focus first on the physical. Age, race, and body size play a big part

Train and work with the best people possible. And most importantly, make sure that those folks truly know what they are doing with songs, monologues (and dance combos)

Research the schools and the programs, EARLY.

As a parent, I think it's wise not to talk incessantly about the three-four most famous musical theatre programs and nothing else really matters. It's just not true. There are many ways to succeed in this field, and every child is different in what will work best for them.

Key words: prepare, organize, pray and encourage!

If we were to do senior year over again, I would NOT have allowed our student to participate in any theatre productions that conflicted with auditions. You will have your whole life to do shows, don't stress yourself out with your school productions, if you can avoid it.

Attend The National Association For College Admission Counseling Performing And Visual Arts College Fair as a sophomore or junior and learn about colleges and meet representatives. The NACAC website lists participating cities.

Resources

College Audition Coach
My web site, collegeauditioncoach.com

Broadway World
All things theatre, broadwayworld.com/

National Association for College Admission Counseling
Performing arts college fair, nacacnet.org

College Confidential
Web site with chat rooms, collegeconfidential.com

Erin Ogren
Independent college counselor, cccollegeconsultants.com

New Dramatists
Source for new playwrights, newdramatists.org

Fair Test
National Center For Fair and Open Testing, fairtest.org/

The Common Application
Colleges that use the common app, commonapp.org/

Karen Kohlhaas
Monologue advice for auditions, monologueaudition.com

National Foundation for the Advancement of the Arts
YoungArts competition, www.youngarts.org

National Association of Teachers of Singing
Singing competition, nats.org

Theatermania U
For theatre everywhere, theatermania.com/tmu/

The National Unified Auditions
Regional BFA college auditions, unifiedauditions.com

Acceptd
Site for most prescreen uploads, getacceptd.com

Kelsey Edwards
Professional head shot photographer, kelseyedwardsphoto.com

The Drama Book Shop
Bookstore for plays, dramabookshop.com

Backstage
Resource for performers, backstage.com

American Theater Magazine
Magazine about all things theater, tcg.org

Playbill
Performing arts trade publication, playbill.com

Dramatics Magazine
High school drama magazine, edta.org

Mental Management
Techniques for staying positive during competition,
mentalmanagement.com

Crawford Performance Solutions
Build mental clarity and confidence, billcphd.com/

Huffington Post
Follow my college blog, huffingtonpost.com/mary-anna-dennard/

Summer Performing Arts Programs

These are suggested summer training programs and websites compiled from College Confidential parents, student contributors and myself. Some require auditions and some do not. Programs vary in length and cost.

CALIFORNIA
American Conservatory Theater Summer Training Congress - http://www.act-sf.org/home/conservatory/summer_training_congress.html

California State Summer School for the Arts - https://www.csssa.org/academic-programs/theater/

Groundlings Comedy Improv-
http://www.groundlings.com/school/teens.aspx
IdyllwildARTS Summer Program - http://www.idyllwildarts.org/page.cfm?p=736

Music Theatre Conservatory - Notre Dame de Namur University -http://www.musictheatreconservatory.org/

Musical Theatre University -
http://www.musicaltheatreuniversity.com/

Second City Comedy Improv-http://www.secondcity.com/courses/hollywood/camps/
University of California, Los Angeles-
http://www.summer.ucla.edu/institutes/ActingandPerformance

University of Southern California-
https://summer.usc.edu/general/summer_seminars_contemptheatre.shtml

COLORADO
American Singer MT Summer Program -
http://www.americansinger.com/

Perry-Mansfield Performing Arts Camp -
http://perry-mansfield.org/:

CONNECTICUT
Buck's Rock Performing and Creative Arts Camp - http://www.
bucksrockcamp.com/

Center for Creative Youth (Wesleyan University) - http://www.crec.
org/ccy/index.php

Yale Explo - Music Theater -
http://www.explo.org/360/yale

DISTRICT OF COLUMBIA
Georgetown University - US Performing Arts Camps - http://www.
usperformingarts.com/nyc-broadwayconservatorycamp.php

FLORIDA
Broward Center for the Performing Arts - http://www.browardcenter.
org/education/student-programs/camp

The Broadway Theatre Project (BTP) -
http://broadwaytheatreproject.com/

National High School Institute (Northwestern University Cherubs)
- http://nhsi.northwestern.edu/theatrearts/

GEORGIA
Broadway Dreams Foundation –
http://mybroadwaydreams.com/

ILLINOIS
The Second City Comedy Improv-
http://www.secondcity.com/

Youth Sing Praise Foundation -
http://youthsingpraise.com/

MASSACHUSETTS
Emerson College Summer Pre College Program - http://www.emerson.
edu/academics/professional-studies/programs-high-school-students/
pre-college-studio-programs/musical-theatre-program

Berklee School Of Music-
https://www.berklee.edu/summer/programs/musical-theater?gclid=C
ODU1OOS2cQCFQaNaQod3mUASQ
The Boston Conservatory Vocal/Choral Intensive - http://www.
bostonconservatory.edu/vocalchoral-intensive-vci

Boston University Summer Theatre Institute (BUSTI) http://www.
bu.edu/cfa/busti/

Vineyard Arts Project Musical Theatre Lab - http://www.
finelinetheatrearts.com/Vineyard.html

Walnut Hill School for the Arts - http://walnuthillarts.org/admission/
summer-programs/summer-theater/

MICHIGAN
Interlochen -
http://www.interlochen.org/

MPulse -
http://www.music.umich.edu/special_programs/youth/mpulse/

Take it from the Top -
http://www.whartoncenter.com/education-engagement/programs-
for-students/take-it-from-the-top

MINNESOTA
Artsbridge -
https://artsbridge.com/

MISSOURI
MUNY/Webster -
http://www.muny.org/eya

NORTH CAROLINA
North Carolina School of the Arts - Summer Session - Drama -http://
www.uncsa.edu/summersession/drama.htm

The Performing Arts Project (TPAP) - http://www.
performingartsproject.com/

NEW JERSEY
Rider University - Summer Music Theatre at Westminster - http://
www.rider.edu/academics/colleges-schools/wca/woce/summer-
camps/music-theater-workshop

Rutgers Summer Acting Conservatory (Mason Gross) -http://
www.masongross.rutgers.edu/content/rutgers-summer-acting-
conservatory

NEW YORK
Broadway Artists Alliance Summer Intensives - http://www.
broadwayartistsalliance.org/programs/summer-intensives/

Camp Broadway - http://www.campbroadway.com/

CAP21 High School MT Training - http://www.cap21.org/cap21/
conservatory/High_School/

Circle in the Square Theatre School - Summer MT Workshop -http://
circlesquare.org/summer_workshops.htm

Columbia University Theatrical Collaboration - http://ce.columbia.edu/
high-school/nyc/junior-senior-courses/theatrical-collaboration-the-
actor-the-director-and-the-playwright

French Woods - http://www.frenchwoods.com/

Ithaca College Summer College (Musical Theatre Performance) -http://www.ithaca.edu/summercollege/threeweek/ threeweekcourses/?item=5676

Lee Strasberg Institute - http://youngactorstrasberg.com/teens-summer-new-york/

Long Lake Camp for the Arts - http://www.longlakecamp.com/ theater-camp.html

Making It on Broadway Intensives - https://www.makingitonbroadway. net/index

NYU Summer High School-http://specialprograms.tisch.nyu.edu/ object/hsnycdrama.html

Open Jar Institute - http://www.openjarinstitute.com/Summer-Institute.html

Pace Summer Scholars http://www.pace.edu/summer-scholars/ courses/musical-theater

Stage Door Manor - http://www.stagedoormanor.com/
Steinhardt - NYU Summer Study in Music Theatre - http://steinhardt. nyu.edu/music/summer/musictheatre

Stella Adler Studio-
http://www.stellaadler.com/classes/teen/
Syracuse University Summer College (Acting & Musical Theater) -http://summercollege.syr.edu/program/acting-musical-theater/

The Broadway Workshop - http://broadwayworkshop.com/

TripleArts - http://www.triplearts.com/

Wagner College - Summer Music Theatre Institute - http://wagner. edu/theatre/smti/

OHIO
BW Overtures - http://www.bw.edu/academics/conservatory/outreach/smp/mth/

UC College Conservatory of Music High School MT Workshop - http://ccm.uc.edu/prep/summer-2015/15immersion/2015-immersion-musical-theatre-workshop.html

OKLAHOMA
Oklahoma City University HS MT Program - http://www.okcu.edu/music/performing-arts-academy/programs/summer/high-school/

PENNSYLVANIA
Carnegie Mellon Summer Pre-College Program - http://admission.enrollment.cmu.edu/pages/pre-college-drama

Penn State Summer Musical Theatre Intensive - http://theatre.psu.edu/summer

University Of The Arts Pre-College Summer Program - http://www.uarts.edu/academics/pre-college-programs/summer-institute-theater

TEXAS
Dallas Summer Musicals College Weekend, http://www.dallassummermusicals.org/HSMA-CollegeSchedule.shtm

TexArts-
http://www.tex-arts.org/academy/summer-camps-15.aspx
Texas Musical Theatre Workshop - http://www.texasmusicaltheatreworkshop.com/:

Texas State University - HS Theatre Camp - http://www.theatreanddance.txstate.edu/Theatre-Programs/Camp-overview/High-school-theatre-camp.html:

VIRGINIA
Torggler Summer Vocal Institute at Ferguson Center for the Arts - http://cnu.edu/tsvinstitute/index.html

WASHINGTON
The 5th Avenue Theatre Summer Program - https://www.5thavenue.
org/education/youth#summer-programs

VARIOUS CITIES ACROSS US

Broadway Dreams Foundation –
http://mybroadwaydreams.com/
Atlanta, Omaha , New York, Los Angeles, Philidelphia

US Performing Arts Camps-
http://www.usperformingarts.com/
Ten US Cities
CANADA
Centauri Summer Arts Camp –
http://www.centauriartscamp.com/

The Second City Comedy Improv
http://www.secondcity.com/courses/toronto/kids/

Stratford Shakespeare Festival - King's Company MT Workshop
http://www.stratfordfestival.ca/education/students.aspx?id=1090

ENGLAND
British American Drama Academy - Midsummer Conservatory
Program -http://www.badaonline.com/programs/midsummer-
conservatory-program/

The Oxford Experience-
https://www.oxford-royale.co.uk/course/new-perspectives
Royal Academy Of Dramatic Art-
https://www.rada.ac.uk/courses/summer-courses/acting-
performance/young-actors-summer-school/course-overview

Colleges Offering Degrees in Acting and Musical Theater

This is a comprehensive (though not complete) list of acting and musical theater degree programs. It includes BA, BFA, and BM offerings. Some require auditions and some do not. It is organized it by region.

West

Arizona
Arizona State University
University Of Arizona

California
California Institute for the Arts
California State University Chico
California State University Fullerton
Chapman College
Loyola Marymount University
Notre Dame de Namur University
Occidental College
Pepperdine University
Santa Clara University
University of California Irvine
University of California Los Angeles
University of Southern California

Colorado
Metropolitan State College of Denver
University of Colorado
University of Northern Colorado

Nevada
University of Nevada Las Vegas

New Mexico
College of Santa Fe
Santa Fe University of Art and Design

Oregon
Southern Oregon University

Utah
Brigham Young University
University of Utah
Weber State University

Washington
University of Puget Sound
Cornish College
Central Washington University

Wyoming
Casper College
University of Wyoming

Midwest
Illinois
Colombia College
DePaul University
Illinois State University

Illinois Wesleyan University
Millikin University
North Central College
Northwestern University
Rockford College
Roosevelt University
Southern Illinois University
University of Illinois Chicago
Western Illinois University

Indiana
Ball State University
Indiana University
Vincennes University
University of Evansville

Iowa
Drake University

Kansas
Friends University
Wichita State University
University of Kansas

Michigan
Central Michigan University
Oakland University
University of Michigan
Wayne State University
Western Michigan University

Minnesota
University of Minnesota, Duluth
University of Minnesota, Guthrie Theater

Missouri
Avila University
Kansas City University
Missouri State University
Missouri Valley College
Southwest Missouri State University
Stephens College
University of Missouri
Webster University
Drake University

Nebraska
Creighton University
Nebraska Wesleyan University
University of Nebraska
University of Nebraska at Kearney

Ohio
Ashland University
Baldwin-Wallace College
Kent State University
Marietta College
Ohio Northern University
Otterbein University
University of Akron
University of Cincinnati, Conservatory of Music
Youngstown State University
Wright State University
Bowling Green State
Heidelberg University

Wisconsin
Carthage College
University Of Wisconsin Stevens Point

University of Wisconsin Green Bay
Viterbo University

South

Alabama
Auburn University
Birmingham-Southern College
University of Alabama
University of Southern Alabama

Arkansas
Ouachita Baptist University

Florida
Florida State University
Jacksonville University
Palm Beach Atlantic University
New World School of the Arts
Rollins College
University of Central Florida
University of Florida
University of Miami
University of Tampa
University of West Florida

Georgia
Brenau University
Shorter College
Valdosta University
Young Harris College

Kentucky
Northern Kentucky University

Western Kentucky University

Louisiana
Louisiana State University
Tulane University

Mississippi
University of Mississippi

North Carolina
Catawba College
East Carolina University
Elon University
Lees-McCrae College
Mars-Hill College
Meredith College
North Carolina School of the Arts
University of North Carolina Chapel Hill
University of North Carolina Pembroke
Western Carolina University

Oklahoma
Oklahoma City University
University of Central Oklahoma
University of Oklahoma
University of Tulsa

South Carolina
Coastal Carolina University
Coker College

Tennessee
Belmont University

Texas
Abilene Christian University
Baylor University
Sam Houston State University
Southern Methodist University
Southwestern University
Saint Edwards University
Texas Christian University
Texas State University
Trinity University
University of Houston
University of Texas at Arlington
University of Texas at Austin
University of North Texas
West Texas A&M University

Virginia
James Madison University
Shenandoah Conservatory
Christopher Newport University
Emory and Henry College

West Virginia
West Virginia Wesleyan College

Northeast

Connecticut
Connecticut College
Hartford Conservatory
University of Hartford, The Hartt School

District of Colombia
American University

Catholic University
Howard University

Maine
University of Southern Maine

Maryland
Goucher College
McDaniel College

Massachusetts
Boston College
Boston Conservatory
Boston University
Brandeis University
Dean College
Emerson College
Northeastern University

New Hampshire
Plymouth State University
University of New Hampshire

New Jersey
Montclair State University
Rutgers University
Westminster College of the Arts at Rider University

New York
Adelphi University
Bard College
Fordham University
Hofstra University
Ithaca College

Long Island University
Marymount Manhattan College
Nazareth College
New York University, Tisch School of the Arts
Sarah Lawrence College
New York University, Steinhardt School of Education
Juilliard School
Pace University
Russell Sage College with NYSTI
State University of New York, Buffalo
State University of New York, Courtland
State University of New York, Fredonia
State University of New York, Geneseo
State University of New York, New Paltz
Syracuse University
University of Buffalo
Vassar College
Wagner College
Manhattanville College

Pennsylvania
Carnegie Mellon University
DeSales University
Marywood University
Muhlenberg College
Pennsylvania State University
Point Park University
Seton Hill University
Susquehanna University
Temple University
University of the Arts
West Chester University
Wilkes University

Rhode Island
Rhode Island College
University of Rhode Island

Vermont
Bennington College
Johnson State College
Middlebury College